THE POWER OF
THREE

THE POWER OF
THREE

A Journey Through God's Word On The # 3

By DELILAH FRANZEL-KEMPERT

ELITE

Xulon Press Elite
2301 Lucien Way #415
Maitland, FL 32751
407.339.4217
www.xulonpress.com

© 2017 by DELILAH FRANZEL-KEMPERT

All rights reserved solely by the author. The author guarantees all contents are original and do not infringe upon the legal rights of any other person or work. No part of this book may be reproduced in any form without the permission of the author. The views expressed in this book are not necessarily those of the publisher.

Unless otherwise indicated, Scripture quotations taken from the Living Bible (TLB). Copyright © 1971 by Tyndale House Foundation. Used by permission of Tyndale House Publishers Inc., Carol Stream, Illinois 60188. All rights reserved.

Printed in the United States of America.

ISBN-13: 9781545612750

ABOUT THE AUTHOR
Delilah Franzel Kempert

Reverend Delilah Kempert is an ordained minister. She is a devout woman of faith, adamant about sharing and defending the Word of God. Encouraging those around her, she allows the Spirit of God to flow through her and inspire all she meets; she has even traveled to Guatemala to share the love of Jesus with those less fortunate. Delilah seeks to help raise up a generation enamored with God's presence, trusting the Holy Scriptures as the path to follow in life to succeed in everyday life and to be filled in your heart soul body mind and spirit with the Word of God. Delilah teaches the Women's ministry at Grace Chapel in Deland Florida In her free time, she likes to spend time in her garden, watch movies, and spend time with her family. Her favorite Bible verse is Jeremiah 33:3 (NKJV), which says, "Call to me, and I will answer you, and show you great and mighty things, which you do not know."

PREFACE

This book came about as I read my daily devotional scriptures from the Living Bible. The Holy Spirit brought to my attention how often the number three was recorded in Scripture. So I went through my Bible, from Genesis to Revelation, and recorded every time the number three was written. (In the Word of God, numbers are important.)

The Trinity functions in three: Father, Son, and Holy Spirit. Each has its own function, but all one God. 1 Thessalonians 5:23: "May the God of peace himself make you entirely pure and devoted to God; and may your spirit and soul and body be kept strong and blameless until that day when our Lord Jesus Christ comes back again."

The number three is recorded 467 times in the Bible. Time is divided into three: the past, present, and future. Through my journey researching the number three and its significance pertaining to the Bible, I hope I can inspire you to take your own journey through the numbers in God's Holy Word.

DEDICATION

This book is dedicated to my husband Ron, who is my best friend and my prayer partner. Over the thirty years of marriage we have shared together, Ron has shown his heart of gold and is a giver to mankind. What God puts together let no man take apart. Ron is a steadfast man of God, strong in his convictions.

I would like to acknowledge my mother, Barbara Sanders Franzel, for always believing in me and bringing me up in the House of God along with my six siblings. Mother is a woman of prayer, wisdom, love and she is a pillar of strength for all of us. She is a faithful servant of the Lord's Army.

My dad was a man of God, a deacon in church, the bus mechanic, the baptismal caretaker, bus driver, youth event organizer, and he did evangelism. He would tell all of his children that we could do anything that we put our minds to! See you again in heaven!

My family support: my sons—Brian, Aaron, and Jimmy; my beautiful daughter's-in-love Jessica and Melanie, my grandson's Preston & Bryce.

Thank you to my sister, Christa Franzel Pini, who has believed in me and has shown full support for this book. Pastor Stephen Smith for giving me the opportunity to teach and preach at Grace Chapel.

I thank my Lord Jesus Christ of Nazareth, the Son of the living God, for guidance. His divine help as He led me to write the book to share the Holy Scripture with the world, all seeds sown shall bring in a harvest.

CONTENTS

The Old Testament 1
Genesis
Exodus
Numbers
Deuteronomy
Joshua
Leviticus
Judges
1 and 2 Samuel
1 and 2 Chronicles
1 and 2 Kings
Ezra
Nehemiah
Esther
Job
Proverbs
Ecclesiastes
Isaiah
Jeremiah
Ezekiel
Daniel
Hosea
Amos
Jonah
Zechariah

The New Testament 45
Matthew
Mark
Luke
John
Acts
1 Corinthians
2 Corinthians
Galatians
1 Timothy
2 Timothy
Hebrews
James
Revelation

The Old Testament

GENESIS

The THIRD branch [A river from the land of Eden flowed through the garden to water it; afterwards the river divided into four branches] is the Tigris which flows to the east of the city of Asher, and the fourth is the Euphrates (Genesis 2:14).

Noah was 500 years old and had THREE sons: Shem, Ham, and Japheth (Genesis 5:32).

Construct a skylight all the way around the ship eighteen inches below the roof; and make THREE decks inside the boat – a bottom, a middle, and upper deck and put a door on the side (Genesis 6:16). Noah was told to build a boat by God.

THREE months later as the waters continued to go down, other mountain peaks appeared (Genesis 8:5).

The names of Noah's THREE sons were Shem, Ham, and Japheth. [Ham is the ancestor of the Canaanites.] From these THREE sons of Noah came all the nations of the earth (Genesis 9:18-19).

By the time Terah was seventy years old, he had THREE sons, Abram, Nahor, and Haran (Genesis 11:26).

Then Jehovah told him [Abram] to take a THREE-year-old heifer, a THREE-year-old female goat, a THREE-year-old ram, a turtledove and a young pigeon (Genesis 15:9).

He [Abraham] suddenly noticed THREE men coming toward him, he sprang up and ran to meet them and welcomed them (Genesis 18:2). He [Jacob] saw in the distance THREE flocks of sheep lying beside a well in an open field waiting to be watered, but a heavy stone covered the mouth of the well (Genesis 29:2).

Again she [Leah] became pregnant and had a son, and named him Levi (meaning "attachment") for she said, "Surely now my husband will feel affection for me, since I have given him THREE sons!" (Genesis 29:34).

He [Laban] gave them to Jacob's sons to take them THREE days distance, and Jacob stayed and cared for Laban's flock (Genesis 30:36).

Laban didn't learn of their [Jacob's wives and sons] flight for THREE days (Genesis 31:22).

But THREE days later, when their wounds were sore and sensitive to every move they made, two of Dinah's brothers, Simeon and Levi, took their swords, entered the city without opposition, and slaughtered every man there (Genesis 34:25).

Esau married THREE local girls from Canaan (Genesis 36:2).

They [Judah and a Canaanite girl a daughter of Shua] lived at Chezib and had THREE sons, Er, Onan, and Shelah (Genesis 38:3).

About THREE months later word reached Judah that Tamar, his daughter-in-law, was pregnant, obviously as a result of prostitution (Genesis 38:24).

"In my dream," he [the butler] said, "I saw a vine with THREE branches that began to bud and blossom, and soon there were clusters of ripe grapes (Genesis 40:10).

"I know what the dream means," Joseph said, "The THREE branches mean THREE days!" (Genesis 40:12).

Within THREE days Pharaoh is going to take you [chief butler] out of prison and give you back your job again as chief butler (Genesis 40:13).

When the chief baker saw that the first dream had such a good meaning, he told his dream to Joseph, too. "In my dream," he said, "There were THREE baskets of pastries on my head" (Genesis 40:6).

The Old Testament

"The THREE baskets mean THREE days," Joseph told him [chief baker]. "THREE days from now Pharaoh will take off your head and impale your body on a pole, and the birds will come and pick off your flesh!" (Genesis 40:18-19).

Pharaoh's birthday came THREE days later and he held a party for all his officials and household staff (Genesis 40:20).

So he [Joseph] threw them [Joseph's brothers] all into jail for THREE days. The THIRD day, Joseph said to them, "I am a God-fearing man and I'm going to give you an opportunity to prove yourselves" (Genesis 42:17-18).

Commentary

God can give us dreams and visions. Listen to what the Spirit of God is saying to you. God gave Joseph the ability to interpret dreams, to bring him from the pit to the palace. As a God-fearing man, Noah was able to save his family from the impending flood.

EXODUS

When the baby's mother saw that he [Moses] was an unusually beautiful baby, she hid him at home for THREE months (Exodus 2:2).

But Aaron and Moses persisted "The God of the Hebrews has met with us," they declared. "We must take THREE days' trip into the wilderness and sacrifice there to Jehovah our God: If we don't obey him we face death by plague or sword." (Exodus 5:3)

We must take a THREE-day trip into the wilderness and sacrifice there to Jehovah our God, as he commanded us (Exodus 8:27).

So Moses did, [lifted his hands toward heaven] and there was thick darkness over all the land for THREE days (Exodus 10:22).

When word reached the King of Egypt that the Israelites were not planning to return to Egypt after THREE days, but to keep going, Pharaoh and his staff became bold again. "What is this we have done, letting all these slaves get away?" they asked (Exodus 14:5).

Then Moses led the people of Israel on from the Red Sea and they moved out into the wilderness of Shur and were there THREE days without water (Exodus 15:22).

The Israelites arrived in the Sinai Peninsula THREE months after the night of their departure from Egypt (Exodus 19:1).

On the morning of the THIRD day there was a terrific thunder and lightning storm, and a huge cloud came down upon the mountain, and there was a long, loud blast from a ram's horn; and all the people trembled (Exodus 19:16).

If he [a man that takes a Hebrew slave] fails in any of these THREE things, [takes another wife and may not reduce her food or clothing or fail to sleep with her as his wife] then she [Hebrew slave] may leave freely without any payment (Exodus 21:11).

There are THREE annual religious pilgrimages you must take (Exodus 23:14).

At these THREE times each year, every man in Israel shall appear before the Lord God (Exodus 23:17).

Then make a table of Acacia wood THREE feet long, one and one-half feet wide and two and one-quarter feet high (Exodus 25:23).

It will have THREE branches going out from each of the center shaft, each branch decorated with THREE almond flowers (Exodus 25:32-33).

On each side of the entrance there will be twenty-two and one-half feet of curtain, held up by THREE posts imbedded in THREE sockets (Exodus 27:14-14).

In the THIRD row [chest piece] will be an amber, an agate, and an amethyst (Exodus 28:19).

With one of them [yearling lambs] offer THREE quarts of finely ground flour mixed with two and one-half pints of oil, pressed from olives, also two and one-half pints of wind, as an offering (Exodus 29:40).

It [altar] is to be eighteen inches square and THREE feet high, with horns carved from wood of the altar – they are not to be merely separate parts that are attached (Exodus 30:2).

And you must remember to celebrate these THREE annual religious festivals: the festival of weeks, the festival of first wheat, and the harvest festival (Exodus 34:22).

The incense altar was made of Acacia wood. It was eighteen inches square and THREE feet high, with its corner horns made as part of the altar so that it was all one piece (Exodus 37:25).

In the THIRD row [chest piece] were a jacinth, an agate, and an amethyst (Exodus 39:12).

Commentary

The world says, "Three strikes and you are out." However, we need to remember to pray for each other. Even Jesus said, "In three days I shall rise." You may not be a person who gives out chances, but remember about patience.
James 5:16: "Admit your faults to one another and pray for each other so that you may be healed."

Luke 9:22: "'For I, the Messiah, must suffer much', he said, 'and be rejected by the Jewish leaders-the elders, chief priests, and teachers of the law-and be killed; and three days later I will come back to life again.'"

The Power Of Three

NUMBERS

On the THIRD day Eliab, the son of Helon, chief of the tribe of Zebulun, came with his offerings – the same as those presented on the previous days (Numbers 7:24).

> So, beginning the day the altar was anointed, it was dedicated by these gifts from the chiefs of the tribes of Israel. Their combined offerings were as follows: twelve silver platters (each weighing about THREE pounds); twelve silver bowls (each weighing about two pounds); (so the total weight of the silver was about sixty pounds); twelve gold trays (the trays weighing about four ounces apiece, so the total weight of gold was about THREE pounds). (Numbers 7:84-86)

> They [at the head of the march was the tribe of Judah, next came the tribe of Issachar and then the tribe of Zebulun and the tribe of Levi carried the Tabernacle upon their shoulders then the camp of Reuben, next the tribe of Simeon, then the tribe of Gad, next came the Kohathites, next in line was the tribe of Ephraim, the tribe of Manasseh and the tribe of Benjamin, last of all were the tribes headed by the flag of the tribe of Dan, the tribe of Asher then the tribe of Naphtali. That was the order in which the tribes traveled] traveled for THREE days after leaving Mount Sinai, with the ark at the front of the column to choose a place for them to stop. (Numbers 10:33)

The Lord sent a wind that brought quail from the sea, and let them fall into the camp and all around it as far as one could walk in a day in any direction, there were quail flying THREE or four feet above the ground (Numbers 11:31).

Immediately [the Lord] he summoned Moses, Aaron and Miriam to the tabernacle: "Come here you THREE," he commanded. So

The Old Testament

they stood before the Lord (Now Moses was the humblest man on earth) (Numbers 12:3-4).

Oh, please, show the great power (of your patience) by forgiving our sins and showing us your steadfast love. Forgive us even though you have said that you don't let sin go unpunished, and that you punish the father's fault in the children to the THIRD and fourth generation (Numbers 14:17-18).

If a lamb is being sacrificed, use THREE quarts of fine flour mixed with THREE pints of oil, accompanied by THREE pints of wine for a drink offering (Numbers 15:4-5).

If the sacrifice is a young bull, then the grain offering accompanying it must consist of nine quarts of fine flour mixed with THREE quarts of oil, plus THREE quarts of wine for the drink offering (Numbers 15:8-10).

One day Korah (son of Izhar, grandson of Kohath, and a descendant of Levi) conspired with Dathan and Abiram (the sons of Eliab) and On (the son of Peleth), all THREE from the tribe of Reuben (Numbers 16:1).

Anyone who touches a dead human body shall be defiled for seven days, and must purify himself the THIRD and seventh days with water (run through the ashes of the red heifer); then he will be purified; but if he does not do this on the THIRD day, he will continue to be defiled even after the seventh day (Numbers 19:11-12).

This shall take place on the THIRD and the seventh days; then the defiled person must wash his clothes and bathe himself, and that evening he will be out from under the defilement (Numbers 19:19).

So Moses did as the Lord had commanded him. The THREE of them [Moses, Aaron, Eleazar] went up together into Mount Hor as all the people watched (Numbers 20:27).

Then the Lord caused the donkey to speak: "What have I done that deserves your beating me these THREE times?" she asked (Numbers 22:28).

"Why did you beat your donkey those THREE times?" the angel demanded. "I have come to stop you because you are headed for destruction. THREE times the donkey saw me and shied away from me; otherwise I would certainly have killed you by now, and spared her." (Numbers 22:32-33)

The Power Of Three

With them [a lamb in the morning and a lamb in the evening, male lambs without defect] shall be offered a grain offering of THREE quarts of finely ground flour mixed with THREE pints of oil (Numbers 28:5).

Along with it shall be the drink offering, consisting of THREE pints of strong wine with each lamb, poured out in the Holy Place before the Lord (Numbers 28:7).

> And for each lamb, THREE quarts of finely ground flour mixed with oil for a grain offering. This burnt offering shall be presented by fire, and will please the Lord very much. Along with each sacrifice shall be a drink offering – six pints of wine with each bull, four pints for a ram, and THREE pints for a lamb. This, then, will be the burnt offering each month throughout the year. (Numbers 28:13-14)

With each bull there shall be a grain offering of nine quarts of fine flour mixed with oil; with the ram there shall be six quarts; and with each of the seven lambs there shall be THREE quarts of fine flour (Numbers 28:20-21).

These shall be accompanied by your grain offering of nine quarts of fine flour mixed with oil with each bull, six quarts with the ram, and THREE quarts with each of the seven lambs (Numbers 28:28-29).

A grain offering of nine quarts of fine flour mingled with oil shall be offered with the bull, six quarts with the ram, and THREE quarts with each of the seven lambs (Numbers 29:3-4).

And their accompanying grain offerings, nine quarts of fine flour mixed with oil are to be offered with the bull; six with the ram; and THREE with each of the seven lambs (Numbers 29:9-10).

And THREE quarts for each of the fourteen lambs (Numbers 29:15).

On the THIRD day of the festival, offer eleven young bulls, two rams, fourteen male yearling lambs, each without defect (Numbers 29:20).

Now stay outside of the camp for seven days, all of you who have killed anyone or touched a dead body. Then purify yourselves and your captives on the THIRD and seventh days (Numbers 31:19).

From there they went through the middle of the Red Sea and on for THREE days into the Etham wilderness, camping at Marah (Numbers 33:8).

THREE of these six cities of refuge are to be located in the land of Canaan, and THREE on the east side of the Jordan River (Numbers 35:13-14).

Commentary

Mothers usually count, "1-2-3," to their children. It's a warning that by the count of the number three, consequences shall take place. God wants us to hearken to His voice, obey His statutes and to love each other.

Numbers is the culmination of the story of Israel's exodus from oppression in Egypt and their journey to take possession of the land God promised their fathers.

DEUTERONOMY

Then Moses instructed the people of Israel to set apart THREE cities east of the Jordan River [Where anyone who accidentally killed someone could flee for safety] (Deuteronomy 4:41).

> You shall not bow down to any images nor worship them in any way, for I am the Lord your God. I am a jealous God, and I will bring the curse of a father's sins upon even the THIRD and fourth generation of the children of those who hate me; but I will show kindness to those who love me and keep my commandments. (Deuteronomy 5:9-10)

Every THIRD year you are to use your entire tithe for local welfare programs (Deuteronomy 14:28).

You must set apart THREE cities of refuge so that anyone who accidently kills someone may flee to safety. Divide the country into THREE districts, with one of these cities in each district, and keep the roads to these cities in good repair (Deuteronomy 19:2-3).

(Whether he does this depends on your obedience to all these commandments I am giving you today – loving the Lord your God and walking his paths), then you must designate THREE additional cities of refuge (Deuteronomy 19:9).

Never convict anyone on the testimony of one witness. There must be at least two and THREE is even better (Deuteronomy 19:15).

Every THIRD year is a year of special tithing. That year you are to give all your tithes to the Levites, migrants, orphans, and widows, so that they will be well fed (Deuteronomy 26:12).

Commentary

Moses wrote the book of Deuteronomy, which is in fact a collection of his sermons to Israel just before they crossed the Jordan. The book of Deuteronomy is not much different from that of Exodus.

JOSHUA

Then Joshua issued instructions to the leaders of Israel to tell the people to get ready to cross the Jordan River. "In THREE days we will go across and conquer and live in the land which God has given us," he told them (Joshua 1:10-11).

"Escape to the mountains," she [Rahab] told them. "Hide there for THREE days until the men who are searching for you have returned; then go on your way." (Joshua 2:16)

The spies went up into the mountains and stayed there THREE days until the men who were chasing them had returned to the city after searching everywhere along the road without success (Joshua 2:22).

On the THIRD day, officers went through the camp giving these instructions: "When you see the priests carrying the Ark of God, follow them." (Joshua 3:2)

THREE days later the facts came out these men were close neighbors. The Israelite Army set out at once to investigate, and reached their cities in THREE days (The names of the cities were Gibeon, Chephirah, Be-Eroth, and Kiriath-Jearim.) (Joshua 9:16-17).

Caleb drove out the descendants of the THREE sons of Anak, Talmai, Sheshai, and Ahiman (Joshua 15:14).

The half-tribes which were situated in the areas assigned to Issachar and Asher, Bethshean, Ible-am, Dor, Endor, Taanach, Megiddo (where there are THREE cliffs), with their respective villages (Joshua 17:11).

Commentary

Let us not forget the three crosses on Calvary. Ask Jesus to forgive you of your sins, come into your heart, and believe He died and arose on the third day for you and is returning again.

The book of Joshua was also God's plan that Israel become a light to the pagan nations and the cause of their salvation.

LEVITICUS

Eat it [peace offering] the same day you offer it, or the next day at the latest; and remaining until the THIRD must be burned (Leviticus 19:6).

For any of it eaten on the THIRD day is repulsive to me, and will not be accepted (Leviticus 19:7).

If you eat it on the THIRD day you are guilty, for you profane the holiness of Jehovah, and you shall be excommunicated from Jehovah's people (Leviticus 19:8).

When you have entered the land and have planted all kinds of fruit trees, do not eat the first THREE crops, for they are considered ceremonially defiled (Leviticus 19:23).

If a man has sexual intercourse with a woman and with her mother it is great evil. All THREE shall be burned alive to wipe out wickedness from among you (Leviticus 20:14).

A grain offering shall accompany it, [a male yearling] consisting of a fifth of a bushel of finely ground flour mixed with olive oil, to be offered by fire to the Lord; this will be very pleasant to him. Also, offer a drink offering consisting of THREE pints of wine (Leviticus 23:13).

Commentary

Father, Son, Holy Spirit. God our Father, Jesus God's Son, the Holy Spirit our guide. Listen to what the Spirit of God says to you. Jeremiah 7:23: "But what I told them was: 'Obey me and I will be your God and you shall be my people; only do as I say and all will be well!'"

JUDGES

The city of Hebron was given to Calab as the Lord had promised: so Calab drove out the inhabitants of the city; they were descendants of the THREE sons of Anak (Judges 1:20).

THREE years later God stirred up trouble between Abimelech and the citizens of Shechem, and they revolted (Judges 9:22-23).

So he [Abimelech] had divided his men into THREE groups hiding in the fields (Judges 9:43).

This was the riddle: "Food came out of the eater, and sweetness from the strong!" THREE days later they [the thirty young men] were still trying to figure it out (Judges 14:14).

"How can you say you love me when you don't confide in me?" she [Delilah] wined. "You've made fun of me THREE times now, and you still haven't told me what makes you so strong!" (Judges 16:15)

Her [a man from the tribe of Levi] father urged him [her husband] to stay while, so he stayed THREE days, and they all had a very pleasant time (Judges 19:4).

So the Israeli army set an ambush all around the village (Judges 20:29).

And went out again on the THIRD day and set themselves in their usual battle for formation (Judges 20:30).

Commentary

Samson was a womanizer, but the Lord used him in spite of his weakness. I believe God can use anyone as long as they are willing.

The Power Of Three

1 SAMUEL

Then, though he [Samuel] was still so small they [Elkanah, Peninnah] took him to the tabernacle in Shiloh, along with a THREE-year-old bull for the sacrifice, and a bushel of flour and some wine (1 Samuel 1:24).

> It was their [Eli's sons] regular practice to send out a servant whenever anyone was offering a sacrifice, and while the flesh of the sacrificed animal was boiling, the servant would put a THREE-pronged fish hook into the pot and demand that whatever it brought up be given to Eli's sons. (1 Samuel 2:13-14)

And the Lord gave Hannah THREE sons and two daughters, meanwhile Samuel grew up in the service of the Lord (1 Samuel 2:21).

So now the Lord called the THIRD time, and once more Samuel jumped up and ran to ELI (1 Samuel 3:8).

"And when you get to the oak of Tabor you will see THREE men coming toward you who are on their way to worship God at the altar at Bethel; one will be bringing THREE young goats, another will have THREE loaves of bread, and the THIRD will have a bottle of wine." (1 Samuel 10:3)

But early the next morning Saul arrived, having divided his army into THREE detachments, and launched a surprise attack against the Amorites and slaughtered them all morning. The remnant of their army was so badly scattered that no two of them were left together (1 Samuel 11:11).

THREE companies of raiders soon left the camp of the Philistines; one went toward Oprah in the land of Shual (1 Samuel 13:17).

Another went to Beth-Horn, and the THIRD moved toward the border above the valley of Zeboim near the desert (1 Samuel 13:18).

Saul had THREE sons, Jonathan, Ishri, and Malchishua; and two daughters, Merab and Michael (1 Samuel 14:49).

The THREE oldest Eliab, Abinadab, and Shammah had already volunteered for Saul's army to fight the Philistines (1 Samuel 17:13).

THREE days later, when David and his men arrived home at their city of Ziklag, they found that the Amalekites had raided the city and burned it to the ground (1 Samuel 30:1).

He [Egyptian youth] had not had anything to eat or drink for THREE days and nights, so they gave him part of a fig cake, two clusters of raisins, and some water, and his strength soon returned (1 Samuel 30:12).

The next day when the Philistines went out to strip the dead, they found the bodies of Saul and his THREE sons on Mount Giboa (1 Samuel 31:8).

Commentary

Three, the Father, the Son, the Holy Spirit all in one accord, function together in unity, just as the Body of Christ should be as one.

The Power Of Three

2 SAMUEL

His [David] second son, Chileab was born to Abigail, the widow of Nabal of Carmel. The THIRD was Absaum, born to Maacah, the daughter of King Talmai of Geshur (2 Samuel 3:3).

It [Ark] remained there for THREE months, and the Lord blessed Obed-edum and all his household (2 Samuel 6:11).

Absalum fled to King Talmai of Geshur (the son of Ammihud) and stayed there THREE years (2 Samuel 13:37).

He cut his hair only once a year, and then only because it weighed THREE pounds, and was too much of a load to carry around (2 Samuel 14:26).

He had THREE sons, and one daughter, Tamar, who was a very beautiful girl (2 Samuel 14:27).

A THIRD were placed under Zeruiah, Joab's brother, Abishai (the son of Zeruiah) and a THIRD under Ittai, the Gittite. The king planned to lead the army himself, but his men objected strongly (2 Samuel 18:2).

"Enough of this nonsense," Joab said. Then he took THREE daggers and plunged them into the heart of Absalom as he dangled alive from the oak (2 Samuel 18:14).

Then the King instructed Amasa to mobilize the army of Judah within THREE days and to report back at that time (2 Samuel 20:4).

So Amasa went out to notify the troops, but it took him longer than the THREE days he had been given (2 Samuel 20:5).

There was a famine during David's reign that lasted year after year for THREE years, and David spent much time in prayer about it. Then the Lord said, "The famine is because of the guilt of Saul and his family, for they murdered the Gibeonites." (2 Samuel 21:1)

One time when David was living in the cave of Adullam and the invading Philistines were at the valley of Rephaim, THREE of the thirty went down at harvest time to visit him (2 Samuel 23:13).

So the THREE men broke through the Philistine ranks and drew water from the well and brought it to David, but he refused to drink it. Instead, he poured it out before the Lord (2 Samuel 23:16).

Of these THREE men, Abishai, the brother he took on THREE hundred of the enemy single-handed and killed them all (2 Samuel 23:18).

The Old Testament

It was by such feats that he [Abishai] earned a reputation equal to the THREE, though he was not actually one of them. But he was the greatest of the thirty, the top-ranking officers of the army, and was their leader (2 Samuel 23:19).

These were some of the deeds that gave Benaiah almost as much renown as the top THREE (2 Samuel 23:22).

"Tell David that I will give him THREE choices." (2 Samuel 24:12)

So God came to David and asked him, "Will you choose seven years of famine across the land, or to flee for THREE months before your enemies, or to submit to THREE days of plague? Think this over and let me know what answer to give God." (2 Samuel 24:13)

So the Lord sent a plague upon Israel that morning, and it lasted for THREE days; and seventy thousand men died throughout the nation (2 Samuel 24:15).

Commentary

David watched Bathsheba bathe and lusted for her then committed adultery. He also knew she had a husband the Hittite Uriah. As a springtime battle came, David ordered Uriah to be murdered. Even though David did these three things, God forgave David and used him.

1 CHRONICLES

Judah had THREE sons by Bath-shua, a girl from Canaan; Er, Onan, and Shelah, but the oldest son Er, was so wicked that the Lord killed him (1 Chronicles 2:3).

Jesse's first son was Elib, his second son was Abinadab, his THIRD son was Shimea (1 Chronicles 2:13).

The THIRD was Absalom, the son of his wife Maacah, who was the daughter of the King Talmai of Geshur (1 Chronicles 3:2).

Neariah had THREE sons Eli-o-enai, Hizkiah, Azrikam (1 Chronicles 3:23).

The sons of Benjamin, according to age were; Bela, the first, Ashbel, the second and Aharah, the THIRD (1 Chronicles 8:1-2).

Azel's brother Eshek had THREE sons; Ulam, the first, Jeush, the second, Eliphelet, the THIRD (1 Chronicles 8:39).

They caught up with Saul and his THREE sons, Jonathan, Abinadab, and Malchishua, and killed them all (1 Chronicles 10:2).

So Saul and his THREE sons died together; the entire family was wiped out in one day (1 Chronicles 10:6).

Their heroic warriors went out to the battlefield and brought back his body and the bodies of his THREE sons. Then they buried them beneath the oak tree at Jabesh and mourned and fasted for seven days (1 Chronicles 10:12).

Jashobeam (the son of a man from Hachon) was the leader of the top THREE – the THREE greatest heroes among David's men. He once killed 300 men with his spear (1 Chronicles 11:11).

The second of the top THREE was Eleazar, the son of Dodo, a member of the subclan of Ahoh (1 Chronicles 11:12).

Another time, THREE of the Thirty went to David while he was hiding in the cave of Adullam. The Philistines were camped in the valley of Rephaim (1 Chronicles 11:15).

He was the chief and the most famous of the Thirty, but he was not as great as the THREE (1 Chronicles 11:21).

He was nearly as great as the THREE, and he was very famous among the Thirty. David made him captain of his bodyguard (1 Chronicles 11:24-25).

Great and brave warriors from the tribe of Gad also went to David in the wilderness. They were experts with both shield and spear and were "lion-faced men," swift as deer upon the mountains. Obadiah was second in command; Eliab was THIRD in command (1 Chronicles 8:9).

They feasted and drank with David for THREE days, for preparations had been made for their arrival (1 Chronicles 12:39).

The Ark remained there with the family of Obededom for THREE months and the Lord blessed him and his family (1 Chronicles 13:14).

> Go and tell David, the Lord has offered you THREE choices, which will you choose? You may have THREE years of famine, or THREE months of destruction by the enemies of Israel or THREE days of deadly plague as the angel of the Lord bring destruction to the land. Think it over and let me know what answer to return to the one who sent me. (1 Chronicles 21:10-12)

Then David divided them [the men of the tribe of Levi] into THREE main divisions named after the sons of Levi – the Gershom division, the Kohath division and the Merari division (1 Chronicles 23:6).

The first toss indicated Joseph of the Asaph clan; the second Gedaliah, along with twelve of his sons and brothers; the THIRD, Zaccur, and the twelve of his sons and brothers (1 Chronicles 25:9).

His sergeants were his sons; Zechariah (the oldest), Jedia-el (the second), Zebadiah (the THIRD), Jathni-el (the fourth), Elam (the fifth), Jeho-hanan (the sixth), Eli-ho-enai (the seventh) (1 Chronicles 26:2-3).

The names of some of his other sons were; Hilkiah, the second; Tebaliah, the THIRD; Zechariah, the fourth. Hosah's sons and brothers numbered thirteen in all (1 Chronicles 26:11).

The commander of the THIRD division was Benaiah. His 24,000 men were on duty the THIRD month of each year (1 Chronicles 27:5).

Commentary

This book lists genealogies in the first nine chapters; chapter ten talks about Saul and his three sons: Jonathan, Abinadab, Malchishua and they all died together in battle. Saul died for his disobedience to God. He consulted a medium and did not ask the Lord for guidance about the battle with the Philistines. Later in the chapters, the Ark of God was brought into the tabernacle. Later, the Philistines were defeated. In the latter chapters, David stepped down from the throne and appointed his son, Solomon, the new King of Israel.

2 CHRONICLES

The tank stood on twelve metal oxen facing outwards; THREE faced North, THREE faced West, THREE faced South, and THREE faced East (2 Chronicles 4:4).

> The number of sacrifices differed from day to day in accordance with the instruments Moses had given; there were extra sacrifices on the Sabbaths, on new moon festivals, and at the THREE annual festivals – the Passover celebration, the festival of weeks, and the festival of tabernacles (2 Chronicles 8:13).

Every THREE years the king sent his ships to Tarshish, using sailors supplied by King Hiram, to bring back gold, silver, ivory, apes, and peacocks (2 Chronicles 9:21).

Rehoboam told them [Jeroboam and friends] to return in THREE days for his decision (2 Chronicles 10:5).

So when Jeroboam and the people returned in THREE days to hear King Rehoboam's decision (2 Chronicles 10:12).

This strengthened the Kingdom of Judah, so King Rehoboam survived for THREE years without difficulty; for during those years there was an earnest effort to obey the Lord as King David and King Solomon had done (2 Chronicles 11:17).

THREE sons were born from this marriage, Jeush, Shemariah, and Zaham (2 Chronicles 11:19).

King Jehoshaphat and his people went out to plunder the bodies and came away loaded with money, garments, and jewels stripped from the corpse so much that it took them THREE days to cart it away (2 Chronicles 20:25).

"This is how we'll proceed: A THIRD of you priests and Levites who come off duty on the Sabbath will stay at the entrance as guards. Another THIRD will go over to the palace, and a THIRD stay in the outer courts of the temple, as required by God's laws." (2 Chronicles 23:4-5)

So all the arrangements were made. Each of the THREE leaders led a THIRD of the priests arriving for duty that Sabbath, and a THIRD of those whose week's work was done and were going off duty – for Jehoiahada the chief priest issued spears and shields to all the army officers (2 Chronicles 23:8).

Jehoiachin was eighteen years old when he ascended the throne, but he lasted only THREE months and ten days, and it was an evil reign as far as the Lord was concerned (2 Chronicles 36:9).

Commentary

The true power comes from the Trinity. The Father, His Son Jesus, and the Holy Spirit. When all three are in motion, *powerful* things happen.

I KINGS

But THREE years later two of Shime-i's slaves escaped to King Achish of Gath. When Shime-i learned where they were, he saddled a donkey and went to Gath to visit the King. And when he had found his slaves, he took them back to Jerusalem (1 Kings 2:39-40).

"Sir," one of them [two young prostitutes] began, "We live in the same house, just the two of us, and recently I had a baby. When it was THREE days old, this women's baby was born too." (1 Kings 3:17-18)

> These rooms were THREE stories high, the lower floor being seven-and-a-half feet wide, the second floor nine feet wide and the upper floor ten-and-a-half feet wide. The rooms were connected to the walls of the Temple by beams resting on blocks built out from the wall – so the beams were not inserted into the walls themselves. (1 Kings 6:6)

The bottom floor of the side rooms was entered from the right side of the Temple, and there were winding stairs going up to the second floor; another flight of stairs led from the second to the THIRD (1 Kings 6:8).

The wall of the inner court had THREE layers of hewn stone and one layer of cedar beams (1 Kings 6:36).

There were forty-five windows in the hall, set in THREE tiers, one tier above the other, five to a tier, facing each other from THREE walls (1 Kings 7:3-4).

The Great Court had THREE courses of hewn stone in its walls, topped with cedar beams, just like the inner court of the Temple and the porch of the palace (1 Kings 7:12).

He cast two hollow bronze pillars, each twenty-seven feet high and eighteen feet around, with THREE-inch thick walls (1 Kings 7:15).

It rested on twelve bronze oxen standing tail to tail. THREE facing North, THREE West, THREE South and THREE East (1 Kings 7:25).

The Power Of Three

"Give me THREE days to think this over," Rehoboam replied. "Come back then for my answer." So the people left (1 Kings 12:5).

So when Jeroboam and the people returned THREE days later, the new King answered them roughly (1 Kings 12:12).

Abijam began his THREE-year reign as King of Judah in Jerusalem during the eighteenth year of Jeroboam's reign in Israel (1 Kings 15:1).

So Baasha replaced Nadab as the King of Israel in Tirzah, during the THIRD year of the reign of King Asa of Judah (1 Kings 15:28).

It was THREE years later that the Lord said to Elijah, "Go and tell King Ahab that I will soon send rain again!" (1 Kings 18:1)

He took twelve stones, one to represent each of the tribes of Israel, and used the stones to rebuild the Lord's altar. Then he dug a trench about THREE feet wide around the altar (1 Kings 18:31-32).

For THREE years there was no war between Syria and Israel. But during the THIRD year, while King Jehoshaphat of Judah was visiting Ahab of Israel (1 Kings 22:1-2).

Commentary

What comes to my spirit is a common middle class home will have three bedrooms, and as the Lord increases you, by your tithing, your home shall increase also. Give and ye shall receive.

The Old Testament

2 KINGS

But they [Prophets of Jericho] kept urging until he [Elisha] was embarrassed, and finally said, "All right, go ahead." Then fifty men searched for THREE days, but didn't find him (2 Kings 2:17).

Meanwhile, when the people of Moab heard about the THREE armies marching against them they mobilized every man who could flight, old and young, and stationed themselves along this frontier (2 Kings 3:21).

"Blood!" they [the people of Moab] exclaimed, "The THREE armies have attacked and killed each other. Let's go and collect the loot!" (2 Kings 3:23)

As a result there was a great famine in the city, and after a long while even a donkey's head sold for fifty dollars and a pint of dove's dung brought THREE dollars (2 Kings 6:25).

He [Jehu] looked up and saw her [Jezebel] at the window and shouted, "Who is on my side?" And two or THREE eunuchs looked out at him (2 Kings 9:32).

Then he [Jehoiada the priest] gave them their instructions: "A THIRD of those who are on duty on the Sabbath are to guard the palace." (2 Kings 11:5-6)

> "Now pick up the other arrows and strike them against the floor." So the King picked them up and struck the floor THREE times. But the prophet was angry with him, "You should have struck the floor five or six times," he exclaimed. "For then you would have beaten Syria until they were entirely destroyed; now you will be victorious only THREE times. (2 Kings 13:18-19)

King Joash of Israel (the son of Jehoahaz) was successful on THREE occasions in reconquering the cities that his father had lost to Ben-hadad (2 Kings 13:25).

Now the land of Israel was filled with Assyrian troops for THREE years besieging Samaria, the capital city of Israel (2 Kings 17:5).

Reigning in Israel at this time: King Hoshea (son of Elah), who had been the King there for THREE years (2 Kings 18:3).

The Power Of Three

THREE years later (during the sixth year of the reign of King Hezekiah and the ninth year of the reign of King Hoshea of Israel) Samaria fell (2 Kings 18:10).

This year my people will eat the volunteer wheat, and use it as seed for next year's crop; and in the THIRD year they will have a beautiful harvest (2 Kings 19:29).

"Go back to Hezekiah, the leader of my people, and tell him that the Lord God of his ancestor David has heard his prayer and seen his tears. I will heal him and THREE days from now he will be out of bed and at the Temple." (2 Kings 20:5)

Meanwhile, King Hezekiah had said to Isaiah, "Do a miracle to prove to me that the Lord will heal me and that I will be able to go to the Temple again THREE days from now." (2 Kings 20:8)

New King of Judah; Jehoahaz; his age when he became King; twenty-three years old; length of his reign, THREE months (2 Kings 23:31).

During the reign of King Jehoiakim, King Nebuchadnezzar of Babylon attacked Jerusalem. Jehoiakim surrendered and paid tribute for THREE years, but then rebelled (2 Kings 24:1).

Length of his reign: THREE months, in Jerusalem; name of his mother: Nehushta (daughter of Elnathan, a citizen of Jerusalem) (2 Kings 24:9).

The general took Seraiah, the Chief Priest, his assistant, Zephaniah, and the THREE temple guards to Babylon as captives (2 Kings 25:18).

Commentary

Elijah the prophet challenged Baal. 2 Kings is where Elijah told Ahab that he had refused to obey God, "Now bring all the people of Israel to Mount Carmel with all of the 450 prophets of Baal and the 400 prophets of Asherah." They are supported by Jezebel. Elijah wanted them not to waiver, follow God or Baal. Elijah told them to bring two young bulls, cut them into pieces, lay them on the wood altar, put fire under the wood, then pray to your god and I will pray to the Lord the God who answers by sending fire to light the wood. He is the true God!

EZRA

There will be THREE layers of huge stones in the foundation, topped with a layer of new timber (Ezra 6:4).

We assembled at the Ahava River and camped there for THREE days while I went over the lists of the people and the priests who had arrived and I found that not one Levite had volunteered (Ezra 8:15).

> Then a proclamation was made throughout Judah and Jerusalem that everyone should appear at Jerusalem within THREE days and that the leaders and elders had decided that anyone who refused to come would be disinherited and excommunicated from Israel. Within THREE days, on the fifth day of December, all the men of Judah and Benjamin had arrived and were sitting in the open space before the Temple; and they were trembling because of the seriousness of the matter and because of the heavy rainfall. (Ezra 10:7-9)

Commentary:

Overview of the book of Ezra: The return of the Jews to the land of Israel under the leadership of Zerubbabel, to the rebuilding of the Temple of Solomon in Jerusalem. Later, the arrival of Ezar in Jerusalem, Ezar reforms religion and government.

NEHEMIAH

THREE days after my arrival at Jerusalem I stole out during the night, taking only a few men with me; for I hadn't told a soul about the plans for Jerusalem which God had put in my heart. I was mounted on my donkey and the others were on foot (Nehemiah 2:11-12).

The laws of God were read aloud to them for two or THREE hours, and for several more hours they took turns confessing their own sins and those of their ancestors, and everyone worshipped the Lord their God (Nehemiah 9:3).

Commentary

Just like Daniel prayed three times at the window, Satan tried to defeat Daniel. God made Daniel victorious. Keep praying to God and He will answer you and you will be victorious also. My commentaries reflect the thoughts I received while writing this book.

ESTHER

It was the THIRD year of the reign of King Ahasuerus, emperor of vast Media-Persia with its one hundred twenty seven provinces stretching from India to Ethiopia (Esther 1:1).

Two or THREE weeks later, Haman called in the King's secretaries and dictated letters to the governors and officials throughout the empire, to each province in its own languages and dialects; these letters were signed in the name of King Ahasuerus and sealed with his ring (Esther 3:12).

"Go and gather together all the Jews of Shushan and fast for me; do not eat or drink for THREE days, night or day; and I and my maids will do the same; and then, though it is strictly forbidden, I will go in to see the King; and if I perish, I perish." (Esther 4:16)

THREE days later Esther put on her royal robes and entered the inner court just beyond the royal hall of the palace, where the King was sitting upon his royal throne.

Commentary

Just as Haman called in the King's secretaries and dictated letters, I also know the Spirit of God has led me to write this study and to use the number three. Esther was chosen by God and was willing to be used to save the Jewish people.

JOB

He had a large family of seven sons and THREE daughters, and was immensely wealthy, for he owned seven thousand sheep, THREE thousand camels, five hundred teams of oxen, five hundred female donkeys, and employed many servants. He was in fact, the richest cattleman in the entire area (Job 1:2-3).

Before this man finished, still another messenger rushed in: "THREE bands of Chaldeans had driven off your camels and killed your servants, and I alone have escaped to tell you." (Job 1:17)

When THREE of Job's friends heard of all the tragedy that had befallen him they got in touch, with each other and traveled from their homes to comfort and console him. Their names were Eliphaz the Temanite, Bildad the Shuhite, and Zophar the Naamathite (Job 2:11).

The THREE men refused to reply further to Job because he kept insisting on his innocence (Job 32:1).

But he was also angry with Job's THREE friends because they had been unable to answer Job's arguments and yet had condemned him (Job 32:3).

Commentary:

"Many are the afflictions of the righteous but the Lord delivers him out of them all" (Psalm 34:19).

PROVERBS

There are THREE things too wonderful for me to understand – no, four! How an eagle glides through the sky, how a serpent crawls upon a rock, how a ship finds its way across the heaving ocean [the growth of love between a man and a girl] (Proverbs 30:18-19).

There are THREE things that make the earth tremble – no, four it cannot stand: a slave who becomes a King, a rebel who prospers, a bitter woman when she finally marries. A servant girl who marries her mistress' husband (Proverbs 30:21-23).

There are THREE stately monarchs in the earth – no, four: the lion, king of the animals, he won't turn aside for anyone. The peacock. The male goat. A King as he leads his army (Proverbs 30:29-31).

Commentary

Proverbs is filled with godly wisdom; it is as a well filled with water waiting to be drawn.

ECCLESIASTES

And one standing alone can be attacked and defeated, but two can stand back-to-back and conquer; THREE is even better, for a triple-braided cord is not easily broken (Ecclesiastes 4:12).

Commentary

The world talks about the third wheel; no one wants to be the third wheel. Two is company, three is a crowd (says the world). Jesus says three is "as a woven cord not easily broke," such as I pray with my mother and sister, and we move heaven. One will have a word, and another a revelation of what we are praying about.

The Old Testament

ISAIAH

Oh, a very few of her people will be left, just as a few stray olives are left on the trees when the harvest is ended, two or THREE in the highest limbs (Isaiah 17:6).

Then the Lord said, "My servant Isaiah, who has been walking naked and barefoot for the last THREE years, is a symbol of the terrible troubles I will bring upon Egypt and Ethiopia." (Isaiah 20:3)

Commentary

Isaiah was a prophet called to the nation of Judah urging people to repent of their sins and forgiveness and salvation comes from God the Father.

JEREMIAH

And whenever Jehudi finished reading THREE or four columns, the King would take his knife, and slit off the section and throw it into the fire, until the whole scroll was destroyed (Jeremiah 36:23).

Commentary

Jeremiah is the longest book in the Bible in terms of words and verses. Jeremiah was known as the weeping prophet. Jeremiah was set-aside before birth to take a message to the nations, urging a change of heart.

EZEKIEL

"Son of dust, take a sharp sword and use it as a barber's razor to shave your head and beard; use balances to weigh the hair into THREE equal parts." (Ezekiel 5:1)

Even if these THREE men were here, the Lord God swears that it would do no good, it would not save the people from their doom. Those THREE only would be saved, but the land would be devastated (Ezekiel 14:16).

Even if these THREE men were in the land, the Lord God declares that they alone would be saved (Ezekiel 14:18).

"Prophesy to them in this way; clap your hands vigorously, then take a sword and brandish it twice, THRICE, to symbolize the great massacre they face!" (Ezekiel 21:14)

These rooms were in THREE tiers, one above the other, with thirty rooms in each tier (Ezekiel 41:60).

The nave of the temple and the Holy of Holies and the entry hall were paneled, all THREE had recessed windows (Ezekiel 41:16).

The rows of rooms behind this building were the inner wall of the court. The rooms were in THREE tiers, overlooking the outer courts on one side, and having a thirty-five-foot strip of inner court on the other (Ezekiel 42:3).

He shall present a meal offering of one half bushel of flour to go with the ram, and whatever amount he is willing for, to go with each lamb. And he shall bring THREE quarts of olive oil for each half bushes of flour (Ezekiel 46:5).

With the young bull, he must bring one half bushel of flour for a meal offering, with the ram, he must bring one half bushel of flour! With the lamb he is to bring whatever he is willing to give, with each half bushel of grain he is to bring THREE quarts of olive oil (Ezekiel 46:7).

"To summarize! At the special feasts and sacred festivals the meal offering shall be one half bushel with the young bull; one half bushel with the ram; as much as the prince is willing to give with each lamb; and THREE quarts of oil with each half bushel of grain (Ezekiel 46:11).

On the north side, with its one-and-one-half mile wall, there will be THREE gates, one named for Reuben, one for Judah and one for Levi (Ezekiel 48:31).

Commentary

The book of Ezekiel reminds us to seek out the Lord in dark times and examine ourselves. We do not want judgments to come upon us for our deeds.

The Old Testament

DANIEL

THREE years after King Jehoiakim began to rule in Judah, Babylon's King Nebuchadnezzar attacked Jerusalem with his armies, and the Lord gave him victory over Jehoiakim (Daniel 1:1).

The King assigned them [young men from the tribe of Juda] the best of food and wine from his own kitchen during their THREE-year training period, planning to make them his counselors when they graduated (Daniel 1:5).

The end of the ten days, Daniel and his THREE friends looked healthier and better nourished than the youths who had been eating the food supplied by the King (Daniel 1:15).

When the THREE-year training period was completed, the Superintendent brought all the young men to the King for oral exams, as he had been ordered to do (Daniel 1:18).

But suddenly, as he was watching Nebuchadnezzar jumped up in amazement and exclaimed to his advisors, "Didn't we throw THREE men into the furnace?" (Daniel 3:24)

Then at Belshazzar's command, Daniel was robed in purple, and a gold chain was hung around his neck, and he was proclaimed THIRD ruler in the Kingdom (Daniel 5:29).

But though Daniel knew about it, he went home and knelt down as usual in his upstairs bedroom, with its windows open toward Jerusalem and prayed THREE times a day, just as he always had, giving thanks to his God (Daniel 6:10).

Then they told the King, "That fellow Daniel, one of the Jewish captives, is paying no attention to you or your law, He is asking favors of his God THREE times a day." (Daniel 6:13)

The second animal looked like a bear with its paw raised, ready to strike. It held THREE ribs between its teeth, and I heard a voice saying to it, "Get up! Devour many people!" (Daniel 7:5)

The THIRD of these strange animals looked like a leopard, but on its back it had wings like those of birds, and it had four heads and great power was given to it over all mankind (Daniel 7:6).

As for the other THREE animals, their kingdoms were taken from them, but they were allowed to live a short time longer (Daniel 7:12).

I asked too, about the ten horns and the little horn that came up afterward and destroyed THREE of the others – the horn with eyes, and the loud, bragging mouth, the one which was stronger than the others (Daniel 7:20).

> His ten horns are ten kings that will rise out of his empire; then another king shall arise, more brutal than the other ten and will destroy THREE of them. He will defy the most high God, and wear down the saints with persecution, and try to change all laws, morals, and customs. God's people will be helpless in his hands for THREE and a half years. (Daniel 7:24-25)

In the THIRD year of the reign of King Belshazzar, I had another dream similar to the first (Daniel 8:1).

In the THIRD year of the reign of Cyrus King of Persia, Daniel (also called Belshazzar) had another vision. It concerned events certain to happen in the future; times of great tribulation – wars and sorrows, and this time he understood what the vision meant (Daniel 10:1).

When the vision came to me (Daniel said later) I had been I mourning for THREE full weeks (Daniel 10:2).

But now I will show you what the future holds, THREE more Persian Kings will reign, to be succeeded by a fourth, far richer than the others, using his wealth for political advantage, he will plan total war against Greece (Daniel 11:2).

With both hands lifted to heaven, he replied, taking oath by him who lives forever and ever, that they will not end until THREE and a half years after the power of God's people has been crushed (Daniel 12:7).

Commentary

Sometimes we pray for three years, three days, three months, or maybe three hours, but as I have seen, I have faith that our God will answer our prayers; maybe not the way we expected, but for our best.

HOSEA

In just a couple of days, or THREE at the most, he will set us on our feet again, to live in his kingdom (Hosea 6:2).

Commentary

Hosea penned this book to let us know our God is loyal to His covenant in spite of Israel's turning to false gods. God has an unwavering and steadfast love for his people. Hosea also warns of those who would turn their backs on God.

AMOS

> "I ruined your crops by holding back the rain THREE months before the harvest. I sent rain on the city, but not another; while the rain fell on one field another was dry and withered. People from two or THREE cities would make their weary journey for a drink of water to a city that had rain, but there wasn't ever enough. Yet you wouldn't return to me," says the Lord. (Amos 4:7-8)

Commentary

When bitterness or rebellion occurs in our lives, we put God on the back burner. However, God is a jealous God, and He desires us to worship and praise Him. God loves us so much that He gave His *only* Son to die for us and our sins.

The Old Testament

JONAH

Now the Lord had arranged for a great fish to swallow Jonah. And Jonah was inside the fish THREE days and THREE nights (Jonah 1:17).

So Jonah obeyed, and went to Nineveh. Now Nineveh was a very large city, with many villages around it, so large it would take THREE days to walk through it (Jonah 3:3).

Commentary

God may tell us to do something, and lead us by His Holy Spirit to fulfill the task, even if we do not understand. Remember, God's ways are not our ways.

ZECHARIAH

The THIRD by white horses and the fourth by dappled greys (Zechariah 6:3).

And I got rid of their THREE evil shepherds in a single month (Zechariah 11:8).

Commentary

Zechariah was a prophet to the people of Judah. He had visions from God that he was to encourage the weak in faith.

The New Testament

MATTHEW

But Jesus replied, "Only an evil faithless nation would ask for further proof; and none will be given except what happened to Jonah the prophet. For as Jonah was in the great fish for THREE days and THREE nights, so I the Messiah, shall be in the heart of the earth THREE days and THREE nights." (Matthew 12:39-40)

Then Jesus called his disciples and said, "I pity these people, they've been here with me for THREE days now, and have nothing left to eat; I don't want to send them away hungry or they will faint along the road." (Matthew 15:32)

Suddenly Moses and Elijah appeared and were talking with him. Peter blurted out, "Sir, it's wonderful that we can be here. If you want me to, I'll make THREE shelters, one for you and one for Moses and one for Elijah." (Matthew 17:3)

One day while they were still in Galilee, Jesus told them, "I am going to be betrayed into the power of those who will kill me, and on the THIRD day afterwards, I will be brought back to life again." (Matthew 17:22-23)

Jesus told him, "The truth is that this very night, before the cock crows at dawn, you will deny me THREE times." (Matthew 26:34)

He returned to them again and found them sleeping, for their eyes were heavy. So he went back to prayer the THIRD time, saying the same thing again (Matthew 26:43-44).

But even though they found many who agreed to be false witnesses, these always contradicted each other. Finally, two men were found who declared, "This man said, I am able to destroy the temple of God, and rebuild it in THREE days." (Matthew 26:60-61)

Then Peter remembered what Jesus had said: "Before the cock crows, you will deny me THREE times" and went away, crying bitterly (Matthew 26:75).

"So! You can destroy the temple and build it again in THREE days can you? Well, then, come on down from the cross if you are the Son of God!" (Matthew 27:40)

That afternoon, the whole earth was covered with darkness for THREE hours, from noon until THREE o'clock. About THREE o'clock, Jesus shouted, "Eli Eli Lama Sabachthani?" Which means, "My God my God, why have you forsaken me?" (Matthew 27:45-46)

And told him "Sir, that liar once said, after THREE days I will come back to life again." (Matthew 27:63)

Commentary

Jesus did come back to life again, He arose three days later. We must remember here on earth it's appointed for man to die, then face judgment.

MARK

They laughed at him in bitter derision, but he told them all to leave, and taking the little girl's father and mother and his THREE disciples, he went into the room where she was lying (Mark 5:40).

He saw that they were in serious trouble, rowing hard and struggling against the wind and waves. About THREE o'clock in the morning he walked out to them on the water, He started past them (Mark 6:48).

"I pity these people," he said, "for they have been here THREE days, and have nothing left to eat." (Mark 8:2)

Then he began to tell them about the terrible things he would suffer, and that he would be rejected by the elders and the chief priests and the other Jewish leaders and be killed and that he would rise again THREE days afterwards (Mark 8:31).

"Teacher, this is wonderful!" Peter exclaimed, "We will make THREE shelters her, one for each of you." (Mark 9:5)

He would say to them, "I, the messiah, am going to be betrayed and killed and THREE days later I will return to life again." (Mark 9:31)

"They will mock me and spit on me and flog me with their whips and kill me; but after THREE days I will come back to life again." (Mark 10:34)

"Peter," Jesus said, "Before the cock crows a second time tomorrow morning you will deny me THREE times." (Mark 14:30)

"We heard him say, I will destroy this temple made with human hands and in THREE days I will build another, made without human hands." (Mark 14:58)

And immediately the rooster crowed the second time, suddenly Jesus' words flashed through Peter's mind. "Before the cock crows twice, you will deny me THREE times," and he began to cry (Mark 14:72).

"Ha! Look at you now!" they yelled at him. "Sure, you can destroy the temple and rebuild it in THREE days! If you're so wonderful, save yourself and come down from the cross." (Mark 15:30)

About noon, darkness fell across the entire land, lasting until THREE o'clock that afternoon (Mark 15:33).

Commentary

Sometimes in life it may appear like a dark cloud hovers over us, but God says the light makes the darkness dissipate.

LUKE

Mary stayed with Elizabeth about THREE months and then went back to her home (Luke 1:56).

THREE days later they finally discovered him, He was in the temple, sitting among the teachers of law, discussing deep questions with them and amazing everyone with his understanding and answers (Luke 2:46).

"Now which of these THREE would you say was a neighbor to the bandits' victim?" (Luke 10:36)

Then teaching them more about prayer, he used this illustration: "Suppose you went to a friend's house at midnight, wanting to borrow THREE loaves of bread!" (Luke 11:5)

From now on families will be split apart, THREE in favor of me, and two against – or perhaps the other way around (Luke 12:52).

And the THIRD day, I will rise again (Luke 18:33).

But the THIRD man brought back only the money he had started with. "I've kept it safe," he said (Luke 19:20).

A THIRD man was sent and the same thing happened. He too was wounded and chased away (Luke 20:12).

But Jesus said, "Peter, let me tell you something. Between now and tomorrow morning when the rooster crows, you will deny me THREE times, declaring that you don't even know me." (Luke 22:34)

The Power Of Three

At that moment Jesus turned and looked at Peter. Then Peter remembered what he had said – "Before the rooster crows tomorrow morning, you will deny me THREE times." (Luke 22:61)

Once more, for the THIRD time, he demanded, "Why? What crime has he committed? I have found no reason to sentence him to death. I will therefore scourge him and let him go." (Luke 23:22)

There all THREE were crucified, Jesus on the center cross, and the two criminals on either side (Luke 23:33).

By now it was noon, and darkness fell across the whole land for THREE hours, until THREE o'clock (Luke 23:44).

He isn't here! He has come back to life again! Don't you remember what he told you back in Galilee, that the Messiah must be betrayed into the power of evil men and be crucified and that he would rise again on the THIRD day? (Luke 24:7)

We had thought that he was the glorious Messiah and that he had come to rescue Israel, and now, besides all this which happened THREE days ago (Luke 24:21).

And he said, "Yes, it was written long ago that the Messiah must suffer and die and rise again from the dead on the THIRD day." (Luke 24:46)

Commentary

On the cross, Jesus and two others were crucified. One of the men asked forgiveness for his sins so he could spend eternity with Jesus. "For the wages of sin is death, but the gift of God is eternal life through Jesus Christ our Lord" (Romans 6:23).

JOHN

"All right," Jesus replied, "this is the miracle I will do for you: Destroy this sanctuary and in THREE days I will raise it up!" (John 2:19)

"What!" they exclaimed, "It took forty-six years to build this temple, and you can do it in THREE days?" (John 2:20)

They were THREE or four miles out when suddenly they saw Jesus walking toward the boat! They were terrified (John 6:19).

This was the THIRD time Jesus had appeared to us since his return from the dead (John 21:14).

Once more he asked him, "Simon, son of John, are you even my friend?" Peter was grieved at the way Jesus asked the question this THIRD time. "Lord you know my heart; you know I am," he said (John 21:17).

Commentary

God knows our heart and our thoughts. We need God to make us pure, heart, soul, body, mind, and spirit.

The Power Of Three

ACTS

Peter and John went to the temple one afternoon to take part in the THREE o'clock daily prayer meeting (Acts 3:1).

About THREE hours later his wife came in, not knowing what had happened (Acts 5:7).

"About that time Moses was born, a child of divine beauty. His parents his him at home for THREE months (Acts 7:20).

He had to be led into Damascus and was there THREE days, blind, going without food and water all that time (Acts 9:9).

While wide awake one afternoon he had a vision. It was about THREE o'clock and in this vision he saw an angel of God coming toward him (Acts 10:3).

The same vision was repeated THREE times. Then the sheet was pulled up again to heaven (Acts 10:16).

Meanwhile as Peter was puzzling over the vision, the Holy Spirit said to him, "THREE men have come to see you." (Acts 10:19)

But God brought him back to life again THREE days later and showed him to certain witnesses God had selected beforehand, not to the general public (Acts 10:40).

This happened THREE times before the sheet and all it contained disappeared into heaven (Acts 11:10).

Just then THREE men who had come to take me with them to Caesarea arrived at the house where I was staying (Acts 11:11).

Then Paul went to the synagogue and preached boldly each Sabbath day for THREE months, telling what he believed and why, and persuading many to believe in Jesus (Acts 19:8).

He was in Greece THREE months and was preparing to sail for Syria when he discovered a plot by the Jews against his life, so he decided to go north to Macedonia first (Acts 20:3).

And as Paul spoke on and on, a young man named Eutychus, sitting on the windowsill, went fast asleep and fell THREE stories to his death below (Acts 20:9).

Watch out! Remember the THREE years I was with you, my constant watch care over you night and day and my many tears for you (Acts 20:31).

THREE days after Festus arrived in Caesarea to take over his new responsibilities, he left for Jerusalem (Acts 25:1).

Near the shore where we landed was an estate belonging to Publius, the Governor of the island. He welcomed us courteously and fed us for THREE days (Acts 28:7).

It was THREE months after the shipwreck before we set sail again, and this time it was in the Twin Brothers of Alexandria, a ship that had wintered at the island (Acts 28:11).

Commentary

Jesus has risen from the dead and all who believe can be saved. This was the message of the gospel in the book of Acts. Glory to God.

1 CORINTHIANS

There are THREE things that remain, faith, hope, and love and the greatest of these is love (1 Corinthians 13:13).

No more than two or THREE should speak in an unknown language, and they must speak one at a time, and someone must be ready to interpret what they are saying (1 Corinthians 14:27).

Two or THREE may prophesy, one at a time, if they have the gift, while all the others listen (1 Corinthians 14:29).

And that he was buried, and that THREE days afterwards he arose from the grave just as the prophets foretold (1 Corinthians 15:4).

Commentary

John 3:16 tells us the one and only truth. If you need Jesus, please ask God to forgive you of your sins, and to come into your heart and receive salvation. God loves us all. He is no respecter of persons.

2 CORINTHIANS

THREE times I was beaten with rods. Once I was stoned. THREE times I was shipwrecked. Once I was in the open sea all night and the whole next day (2 Corinthians 11:25).

THREE different times I begged God to make me well again (2 Corinthians 12:8).

> Now I am coming to you again, the THIRD time; and it is still not going to cost you anything, for I don't want your money, I want you! And anyway, you are my children and little children don't pay for their fathers' and mothers' food, it's the other way around; parents supply food for their children. (2 Corinthians 12:14)

This is the THIRD time I am coming to visit you. The scriptures tell us that if two or THREE have seen wrong, it must be punished. Well, this is my THIRD warning, as I come now for this visit (2 Corinthians 13:1).

Commentary

"Three Blind Mice," another children's song. As we walk each day, breathe each breath, we need to ask God to open our blind eyes and open our ears so we can hear what the Spirit of God is saying.

GALATIANS

It was not until THREE years later that I finally went to Jerusalem for a visit with Peter, and stayed there with him for fifteen days (Galatians 1:18).

Commentary

Family is a way to open doors to Jesus and salvation. We are God's voice and the sword of the Lord we fight with, His Word, is truth and is our salvation.

1 TIMOTHY

Don't listen to complaints against the pastor unless there are two or THREE witnesses to accuse him (1 Timothy 5:19).

Commentary

In everyday life, even at the scene of a major accident, there are usually different people who witnessed the accident and they are all from different perspectives. That's why we need to witness what we see and know. We need to be witnesses for the salvation of our world.

2 TIMOTHY

Think over these THREE illustrations, and may the Lord help you to understand how they apply to you (2 Timothy 2:7).

Commentary

Timothy was to endure hardship as a good solider. No good solider would give up because some hardship came their way. If you are engaged in war, you cannot be concerned with the affairs of this life. Jesus is our commanding officer.

HEBREWS

A man who refused to obey the laws given by Moses was killed without mercy if there were two or THREE witnesses to his sin (Hebrews 10:28).

Moses' parents had faith too. When they saw that God had given them an unusual child, they trusted God would save them from death and they hid him for THREE months, and they were not afraid (Hebrews 11:23).

Commentary

Trust the Lord to answer your prayers that are in His will for your life and purpose. It may take three minutes, three hours, three days, sometimes three weeks, or even three years. Hold on strong to your faith.

JAMES

Elijah was as completely human as we are, and yet when he prayed earnestly that no rain would fall, none fell for the next THREE and one half years (James 5:7).

Commentary

Daniel prayed three times by his window, and when the time came for the king's fury, God spared Daniel's life. We need to remember to pray and to do what God tells us, God will cover our backs. I use the references of the number three from different stories in the Bible.

REVELATION

The first of these living beings was in the form of a lion; the second looked like an ox; the THIRD had the face of a man and the fourth, the form of an eagle with wings spread out as though in flight (Revelation 4:7).

When he had broken the THIRD seal, I heard the THIRD living being say, "Come," and I saw a black horse, with its rider holding a pair of balances in his hand (Revelation 5:6).

And a voice from among the four living beings said, "A loaf of bread for twenty dollars, or THREE pounds of barley flour, but there is no olive oil or wine." (Revelation 6:6)

The THIRD angel blew, and a great flaming star fell from heaven upon a THIRD of the rivers and springs (Revelation 8:10).

As I watched, I saw a solitary eagle flying through the heavens crying loudly, "Woe, woe, woe to the people of the earth because of the terrible things that will soon happen when the THREE remaining angels blow their trumpets." (Revelation 8:13)

Then a THIRD angel followed them shouting, "Anyone worshipping the creature from the sea and his statue and accepting his mark on the forehead or the hand." (Revelation 14:9)

The THIRD angel poured out his flask upon the rivers and springs and they became blood (Revelation 16:4).

And I saw THREE evil spirits disguised as frogs leap out of the mouth of the dragon, the creature, and his false prophet (Revelation 16:3).

The great city of Babylon split into THREE sections, and the cities around the world fell in heaps of rubble; and so all of Babylon's sins were remembered in God's thoughts, and she was punished to the last drop of anger in the cup of wine of the fierceness of His wrath (Revelation 16:19).

The city itself was pure, transparent gold like glass! The wall was made of jasper, and was built on twelve layers of foundation of stones inlaid with gems: The first layer with jasper, the second with sapphire; the THIRD with chalcedony (Revelation 21:18-21).

The Power Of Three

Commentary

Revelation, the last book in the Bible, gives us a glance of the things that must take place before the return of our Savior. It pulls back the veil of heaven to reveal God's masterpiece.
I pray this book has blessed you and opened your eyes to see what the Spirit of God has shown me about the *power* of the number three. A few of my favorite scriptures:
Matthew 27:63: "After three days I will come back to life again."
Matthew 28:2:

> Suddenly there was a great earthquake; for an angel of the Lord came down from heaven and rolled a side the stone and sat on it. His face shone like lighting and his clothing was brilliant white. The guards shook with fear when they saw him and fell into a dead faint. Then the angel spoke to the woman. "Don't be frightened!" he said. "I know you are looking for Jesus, who was crucified, but He isn't here! For He has come back to life again, just like He said He would."

Matthew 28:45: "That afternoon, the whole earth was covered with darkness for three hours, from noon until three o'clock."
Three is the number of perfection: Father, Son, and Holy Spirit.
Love in Christ our Lord,
Delilah Franzel Kempert

www.ingramcontent.com/pod-product-compliance
Lightning Source LLC
LaVergne TN
LVHW022000060526
838201LV00048B/1644